A New True Book

HOLIDAYS
AROUND THE WORLD

By Carol Greene

This "true book" was prepared
under the direction of
Illa Podendorf,
formerly with the Laboratory School,
University of Chicago

 CHILDRENS PRESS, CHICAGO

This book is for Angela.

Parade

PHOTO CREDITS

Ray Hillstrom—2, 7 (2 photos), 10 (top), 13 (bottom), 34 (bottom left), 44, (top left, bottom right), 45 ©Norma Morrison—29 (2 photos)

A-Stock Photo Finder: ©David Honor—21 (2 photos at top); ©David J. Maenza—4, 13 (top, middle right), 22 (2 photos), 27, 31 (2 photos), 33, 34 (bottom right)

©John Babcock—Cover

Japan National Tourist Organization—21 (bottom)

James P. Rowan—8

Karen Jacobsen—43

Robert J. Serbins, City of Chicago—10 (bottom), 17, 24, 44 (bottom left)

Sheldon Millman—39 (bottom)

Tony Freeman—13 (middle left), 44 (top right)

Religious News Service Photo—15, 19, 26, 37, 40

James L. Kilcoyne—16, 34 (top), 39

Cover—Fireworks

Library of Congress Cataloging in Publication Data

Greene, Carol.
  Holidays around the world.

  (A New true book)
  Includes index.
  Summary: Describes briefly various holidays celebrated throughout the world.
  1. Holidays—Juvenile literature. [1. Holidays]
I. Title.
GT3933.G73 1982   394.2'6   82-9734
ISBN 0-516-01624-5   AACR2

TABLE OF CONTENTS

Circus parade marches down a city street

HOLIDAYS ALL OVER

All over the world people have holidays. Some holidays honor special people. Some holidays remember special events in history.

Some days celebrate special times. The beginning of a new year or harvest time can be a holiday.

Religious holidays are important, too. But there are some holidays, such as April Fool's Day, that are just for fun.

Sometimes many countries celebrate the same holiday, such as

In many parts of the world Christmas trees and Santa Claus costumes are a part of the Christmas celebrations.

Christmas or Easter or New Year's Day. But most countries have their own holidays, too, such as Australia Day or Victoria Day in Canada.

Birthdays are special holidays.

Some days are important only to a few people but not a whole country. Birthdays and anniversaries are that sort of holiday. Do you have any important holidays?

SPECIAL DAYS
IN HISTORY

Countries have birthdays, too. These days are often holidays.

People in Australia celebrate Australia Day on January 26. On this day in 1788, Captain Arthur Phillip landed in Australia.

National costumes and flags are part of every national holiday.

In Canada people celebrate Dominion Day on July 1. In Puerto Rico, July 25 is the country's birthday. Mexico's birthday is on September 16.

The United States has its birthday on July 4. This is called Independence Day.

June 14 is Flag Day in the United States. On this day in 1777, the United States adopted its first official flag.

Another important
birthday is Pan-American
Day on April 14. This day
is important to the
countries of North, Central,
and South America.

All over the world people
celebrate their special
days with fireworks, music,
parades, and speeches.

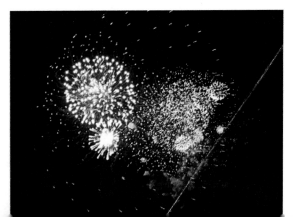

DAYS FOR SPECIAL PEOPLE

The United States has special days for special people. The third Monday in February is George Washington's birthday. He was the first president of the United States.

February 12 is Abraham Lincoln's birthday. He was one of America's greatest presidents.

Many countries remember their heroes with special ceremonies. The family and friends of Martin Luther King, Jr. visit his grave on the anniversary of his death.

On January 15, people remember Dr. Martin Luther King, Jr. He worked hard for equal rights for everyone.

Dressed in their native costumes, these Italians celebrate Columbus Day.

In 1492, Christopher Columbus came to the New World. People in the United States and other parts of North and South America now celebrate Columbus Day on October 12 or on the second Monday in October.

Many cities have a parade on St. Patrick's Day.

Many countries celebrate St. Patrick's Day on March 17. St. Patrick is very important in Ireland. Irish people—and some people who aren't—wear green on St. Patrick's Day. They also have parades and special parties.

17

In Canada, people call the first Monday before May 25 Victoria Day. (May 25 was Queen Victoria's birthday.) On Victoria Day, Canadians celebrate.

In Mexico, December 12 is the day of Our Lady of Guadalupe. This is an important religious day as well as a national holiday.

Procession in honor of St. John the Baptist.

St. John the Baptist's Day is a holiday in Puerto Rico. It falls on June 24. The capital of Puerto Rico, San Juan, is named after St. John the Baptist.

Countries also have days to honor special groups of people. On the second Sunday in May, Americans honor mothers. On the third Sunday in June, they honor fathers. American Indian Day is a holiday in some states. And on May 5, people in Japan celebrate Children's Day!

Above: American Indians
Below: Paper kites are flown on Children's Day in Japan.

On national holidays many families go to the zoo or have an outdoor picnic.

Many countries have days to honor working people. Canada and the United States both celebrate Labor Day on the first Monday in

September. The Soviet
Union calls May 1 and 2
International Labor Days.

Countries also have days
to remember people who
have died. Canada
remembers its war dead
on November 11,
Remembrance Day.

In the United States,
November 11 is called
Veterans Day. It honors all
people who served their

country in the armed forces. The United States remembers its war dead on Memorial Day. That's the last Monday in May.

Australia and New Zealand honor their people who died in the two World Wars on April 25, Anzac Day.

SPECIAL TIMES OF YEAR

There are many kinds of new years. Some are religious and some aren't. Some are big public holidays and some aren't. The first day of school begins a new year for most students. A birthday can be the start of a new year, too.

The Jewish new year is in the fall. It is called Rosh Hashanah. It is a quiet time, but not a sad one.

On Rosh Hashanah the ram's horn is blown.

Statue of
Buddha

Buddhists begin their
new year in the middle of
April. It's called Songkran.
In Thailand people wash
the statues and pictures of
Buddha at this time.

The Hindu new year, Baisakhi, is in April or May. Hindus in India take baths in sacred water to protect themselves from evil.

The Christian new year is called Advent. It begins on the fourth Sunday before Christmas. It is a time of waiting and getting ready.

The Muslim new year is in January or February. It

A Chinese New Year parade

is called Moharram. In India, men and boys do special dances.

Celebrations of the Chinese new year, Yüan Tan, go on for five days.

January 1 is New Year's Day for many countries. In Denmark, young people bang on their friends' doors. They are "smashing in" the new year. In Italy, children sometimes get gifts of money.

In Japan, a gong rings 108 times at midnight. In Burma and Madagascar, people pour water on their heads. They want to start the new year fresh.

In North America many people watch
football games on New Year's Day.

In many countries people
go to parties, and wish
their friends, "Happy New
Year!"

Spring is also a special
time of year. Muslims call
the first day of spring
Basanth. In Pakistan,
Muslims celebrate this day
with kite-flying contests.

31

Hindus have a spring festival called Holi. In India, Hindu children squirt pistols full of red or orange water.

The first day of spring is called the New Year of Trees by Jewish people everywhere. It is an important holiday in Israel.

Dancers in a spring festival in Poland.

May 1 is still called May Day in many countries. In Sweden, some young men pretend to be summer. Others pretend to be winter. Then they have a pretend battle. Of course winter always loses!

33

Above: Students take part in a Thanksgiving Day party.
Below left: A good harvest is a good reason to celebrate.
Below right: Good food is a part of the German Octoberfest.

In the fall, crops are harvested and people give thanks. In the United States, Thanksgiving Day is the fourth Thursday in November. In Canada, it is the second Monday in October. People in both countries eat turkey, vegetables, and fruit. Some go to church.

People in the Virgin Islands celebrate Thanksgiving in November. But they also give thanks on October 25 if there have been no hurricanes that year. Then they pray there won't be any next year.

At Sukkoth Jewish youth build a booth to celebrate the harvest.

Jewish people celebrate
Sukkoth in September or
October. For eight days
they give thanks.

SPECIAL RELIGIOUS DAYS

All religions have their own holidays. (The word "holiday" first meant "holy day.")

For Christians, Christmas and Easter are very important.

For Jewish people, Hanukkah and Passover are special times. Hanukkah is usually in December. Passover is in the spring.

Above: Christian children recall the birth of Jesus Christ.
Below: Jewish children light candles as
part of their Hanukkah celebration.

Muslims pray and fast for a month before they celebrate Ramadan.

Muslims have five important holidays. Maulid is the birthday of the prophet Muhammad. Ramadan is a time for trying to become a better person.

DAYS JUST FOR FUN

Some holidays are just for fun. Groundhog Day is one of those holidays in the United States. People say that if the groundhog sees his shadow on February 2, there will be six more weeks of winter.

February 14 is Valentine's Day in the United States. Many people give cards and gifts to their friends and family.

In Denmark, young people give each other friendship gifts on February 14. The gifts are pressed snowdrops (a spring flower) and poems the young people have made up.

April 1 is April Fool's Day in the United States and other countries. On this day people play silly jokes on one another. Sometimes their ears turn purple. (April Fool!)

October 31 is Halloween.
In the United States
children dress up in
costumes and go from
house to house asking for
treats. Sometimes they
collect money for UNICEF.
That's a group that helps
children all over the world.

Decorated floats, fireworks, costumes, marchers, and bands are part of holiday celebrations all over the world.

IMPORTANT TIMES

Holidays are important
for people everywhere.
They help us honor special
events and special people.
They help us remember
the things we believe in.
And holidays are a great
way for people to get
together and have a good
time!

WORDS YOU SHOULD KNOW

adopt(ah • DOHPT) — to accept in an official way

anniversary(an • ih • VER • sri) — the return each year of the date on which an event happened

celebrate(SELL • ih • brate) — to honor a special occasion

event(e • VENT) — something that happens

harvest(HAR • vist) — to gather in the crop

history(HISS • tory) — a record of past events

holiday(HOL • ih • day) — a special day to celebrate an important date or person

honor(ON • er) — special respect

independence(in • dih • PEN • dence) — not controlled by others

national(NASH • uh • nel) — to involve a nation as a whole

official(oh • FISH • ill) — to be recognized or picked by the proper people

sacred(SAY • krid) — holy; to treat with special respect

UNICEF(YOO • nih • sef) — United Nations Children's Emergency Fund.

veteran(VET • rin) — a person who has served in the armed forces

INDEX

About the Author

Carol Greene has written over 20 books for children, plus stories, poems, songs, and filmstrips. She has also worked as a children's editor and a teacher of writing for children. She received a B.A. in English Literature from Park College, Parkville, Missouri, and an M.A. in Musicology from Indiana University. Ms. Greene lives in St. Louis, Missouri. When she isn't writing, she likes to read, travel, sing, do volunteer work at her church—and write some more. Her The Super Snoops and the Missing Sleepers *and* Sandra Day O'Connor, First Woman on the Supreme Court *have also been published by Childrens Press.*

DATE DUE

Metro Litho
Oak Forest, IL 60452
